D0722774

Backyard Animals
Mice

Leia Tait

Weigl Publishers Inc.

Published by Weigl Publishers Inc.
350 5th Avenue, Suite 3304, PMB 6G
New York, NY 10118-0069
Website: www.weigl.com

Library of Congress Cataloging-in-Publication Data

Tait, Leia.
 Mice / Leia Tait.
     p. cm. -- (Backyard animals)
 Includes index.
 ISBN 978-1-60596-080-7 (hard cover : alk. paper) -- ISBN 978-1-60596-081-4 (soft
cover : alk. paper)
 1. Mice--Juvenile literature. I. Title.

 QL737.R6T14 2010
 599.35'3--dc22

                                        2008052059

Printed in China
1 2 3 4 5 6 7 8 9 0 13 12 11 10 09

Editor Heather C. Hudak
Design Terry Paulhus

All of the Internet URLs given in the book were valid at the time of publication.
However, due to the dynamic nature of the Internet, some addresses may have
changed, or sites may have ceased to exist since publication. While the author
and publisher regret any inconvenience this may cause readers, no responsibility
for any such changes can be accepted by either the author or the publisher.

Photo Credits

Every reasonable effort has been made to trace ownership and to obtain
permission to reprint copyright material. The publishers would be pleased
to have any errors or omissions brought to their attention so that they may
be corrected in subsequent printings.

Weigl acknowledges Getty Images as its primary photo supplier for this title.

Contents

Meet the Mouse

A mouse is a small animal that scurries along the ground. It has a pointed snout, a thin tail, and large, round ears. A mouse's body is covered in short, thick fur that is often brown or gray.

Mice are rodents. Rodents are **mammals** that have sharp front teeth. They use their teeth to gnaw on food and other things, such as wood. Beavers, porcupines, rabbits, rats, and squirrels are also rodents. Nearly half of all mammals on Earth are rodents.

Mice are often mistaken for rats. The main difference between mice and rats is their size. Mice are smaller than rats. In fact, mice are the world's smallest rodents. Most mice are only about 4 to 8 inches (10 to 20 centimeters) long from the tip of their nose to the end of their tail.

Mice are nocturnal. This means they are most active at night.

Mice live in nearly all parts
of the world, except Antarctica.

All about Mice

There are hundreds of mice **species**. The best known is the house mouse. It is about 4 inches (10 cm) long and has dusty-gray fur. The house mouse is found in most parts of the world, wherever there are people. In North America, most of the mice living in cities are house mice.

Outside of cities, the most common mouse in North America is the North American deer mouse. These mice are about 5 to 8 inches (13 to 20 cm) long. They have large ears and black eyes. Their fur is grayish-brown on the back and tail, and white on the belly, legs, and underside of the tail.

Mice can be found in all types of environments, such as deserts, fields, forests, swamps, and mountain ranges.

Where Mice Live

House Mouse

- Found throughout North America in cities, towns, and almost any place people live

White-footed Mouse

- Lives throughout the United States, Canada, and Mexico

North American Deer Mouse

- Found in forests, scrubland, **tundra**, grasslands, and deserts from Canada to Mexico

Eurasian Harvest Mouse

- Lives in Europe and Asia

Mouse History

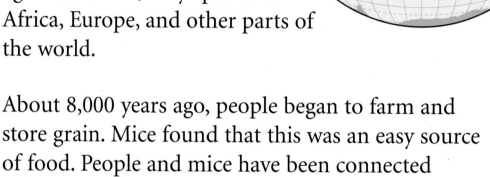

The first mice lived in Asia more than 11 million years ago. Over time, they spread to Africa, Europe, and other parts of the world.

About 8,000 years ago, people began to farm and store grain. Mice found that this was an easy source of food. People and mice have been connected ever since.

When settlers traveled to new places, mice would make their way on board ships that crossed the world's oceans. This is how the house mouse came to North America from Europe in the 1600s.

Mice can run at speeds of up to 7.5 miles (12 kilometers) per hour.

Mice use their long, sensitive whiskers to feel their way in the dark.

Mouse Shelter

Most mice build nests in hollow logs or other protected places. The nests are made from plant matter and are lined with fur, feathers, and paper. Some mice **burrow** underground or climb into trees. House mice build nests between walls and in unused spaces in houses and buildings.

Mice are territorial. This means they claim the area around their nest and defend it from intruders. This area is called their home range. Most mice do not travel more than 50 feet (15 meters) from the nest. If there is a great deal of food nearby, the range will be smaller.

A male mouse will allow a female into his range to form a family group. He will chase away other males.

A mouse will spend its entire life in its home range. It will only move if food runs out or if there is poor weather.

Mouse Features

All mice share the same basic features. Keen hearing tells mice when other animals are nearby. The color of a mouse's fur helps it blend in with its surroundings. Strong legs and feet allow mice to move quickly. Their small size helps them hide in hard-to-reach places.

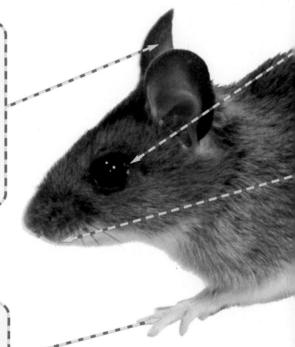

EARS
Mice have large ears and can hear very well. They can hear high-pitched sounds humans cannot hear. This helps mice to communicate, find food, and keep safe from **predators**.

FRONT LEGS
Mice have short front legs with small paws. They use their paws like hands to hold food.

EYES

Mice have poor eyesight. This is because they are most active at night. They use their whiskers to sense their surroundings. Mice have large eyes that help them see at night.

TEETH

Mice have 16 teeth. The four front teeth are **incisors**. These sharp, chisel-shaped teeth never stop growing. Mice wear down their incisors by gnawing food and other objects. A mouse's back teeth are called cheek teeth. They are used for chewing.

TAIL

Mice have long tails that help them balance. A mouse's tail can be as long as its head and body combined. The tail has smooth scales of skin. It is covered in a thin layer of fur.

What Do Mice Eat?

Mice are omnivores. This means they eat both meat and plants. Indoors, mice will eat almost anything humans eat, as well as glue, leather, wood, and soap. In nature, mice eat mostly plants. They prefer seeds, grains, nuts, and fruits.

After mice eat, they keep extra food in their cheeks. They bring it back to their nests to store. In autumn, mice eat and store more food than usual. The stored food is called a hoard. In winter, food is harder to find. Mice live off their hoard. They also search for food under the snow.

Mice will hunt insects, centipedes, and snails.

The white-footed mice eats about one-third of its body weight in food each day.

Mouse Life Cycle

Different types of mice breed at many times during the year. House mice breed year round. They have between five and ten **litters** per year. Females carry their young for about three weeks before giving birth. They have about six young in each litter.

Birth

Baby mice are called pinkies. Except for whiskers on their noses, newborn pinkies have no fur. They cannot hear, and their eyes are closed. Pinkies weigh about 0.04 ounces (1 gram). Young pinkies constantly drink milk from their mother.

One to Seven Weeks

Young mice grow quickly. In one week, pinkies grow fur and double in size. After two weeks, they open their eyes and begin moving around. At three to four weeks of age, pinkies stop drinking their mother's milk. They spend the next few weeks searching for food near the nest.

In nature, most mice only live for about four months. This is because they face many predators, including cats, coyotes, foxes, owls, skunks, snakes, and weasels.

Adult

At eight weeks, mice are fully grown. They can have their own pinkies. They leave their mother's nest to build their own. An adult male is called a buck. An adult female is called a doe.

Encountering Mice

During the day, mice sleep or hide from predators. You are more likely to see a mouse at night. Drumming, rustling, or chirping sounds in grass or bushes may be mice. Indoors, mice may be heard scratching and gnawing between the walls. Droppings are another sign that mice are nearby. Mouse droppings look like tiny black seeds. To avoid attracting mice, keep kitchens clean and place food in containers that mice cannot gnaw.

Mice are important in nature. They eat weeds and insects. They are also a source of food for many animals. However, mice can cause damage with their gnawing. They may also spread diseases, so it is best to avoid handling mice.

Useful Websites

To learn more about mice, visit www.animalcorner.co.uk/pets/ mice/mice_about.html.

To escape from predators, mice run in a zigzag pattern. This makes them more difficult to catch.

Myths and Legends

In ancient times, mice were often thought to be special animals. According to one legend, a kingdom in Egypt was attacked. The king fell asleep, and a god told him in a dream that help would come. That night, mice gnawed through the enemies' weapons and shields. The attack was stopped.

In ancient Rome, mice were linked to the god Apollo. Apollo was sometimes called "Apollo, Lord of Mice." White mice lived under the altars in Apollo's temples. They were cared for by priests and fed special foods.

In ancient Egypt and China, mice were used to predict the future. They were also kept as good luck charms.

A Mouse Legend

Once, a town mouse paid a visit to his cousin, the country mouse. The country mouse loved his cousin and made him welcome. All that the country mouse had to eat was beans, bacon, cheese, and bread. He shared his food with the town mouse. The town mouse pushed the food away. He told his cousin that they could find much better food in town.

The two mice set off. They arrived at the town mouse's home late at night. The pair went to a grand dining room, where they found the remains of a feast. Soon, the two mice were eating jellies and cakes. Suddenly, they heard growling and barking. The door flew open, and in came two huge dogs. The mice ran for their lives.

When they were safe, the country mouse said goodbye to his cousin. He left for the country where the food was not as good but he was safe.

Frequently Asked Questions

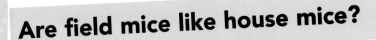

Are field mice like house mice?

Answer: Field mice are actually voles. These are small rodents that belong to their own group in the mouse family. They look like mice, but have smaller eyes, shorter tails, and ears that are nearly hidden in their fur.

Do mice love to eat cheese?

Answer: Mice will eat cheese, but it is a myth that they like it better than other foods. Mice prefer to eat foods that are high in sugar, such as berries, cereal, and chocolate.

Do mice make good pets?

Answer: Mice that live in nature do not make good pets. They may carry diseases that are harmful to humans and animals. **Domestic** mice make great pets. They come in many colors. These mice are larger than mice in nature and live longer. Pet mice should be bought at a pet store.

Puzzler

See if you can answer these questions about mice.

1. What do mice, beavers, porcupines, rabbits, rats, and squirrels have in common?
2. What is the best-known species of mouse?
3. How fast can mice run?
4. How long does it take for mice pups to open their eyes?
5. Which Roman god was linked to mice?

Answers: 1. They are all rodents. 2. the house mouse 3. up to 7.5 miles (12 km) per hour 4. two weeks 5. Apollo

Find Out More

There are many more interesting things to learn about mice. If you would like to learn more, look for these books at your library.

Pascoe, Elaine. *Mice*. Thomson Gale, 2005.

Royston, Angela. *Mouse*. DK Preschool, 2008.

Words to Know

burrow: to dig a hole or tunnel in the ground

domestic: used to living in the care of humans

incisors: front teeth that are used for cutting

litters: groups of animals born at the same time

mammals: warm-blooded animals with a backbone and hair, whose young are fed with their mother's milk

predators: animals that hunt other animals for food

species: a group of living things that can breed with one another

tundra: flat, treeless places where the ground remains frozen all year

Index